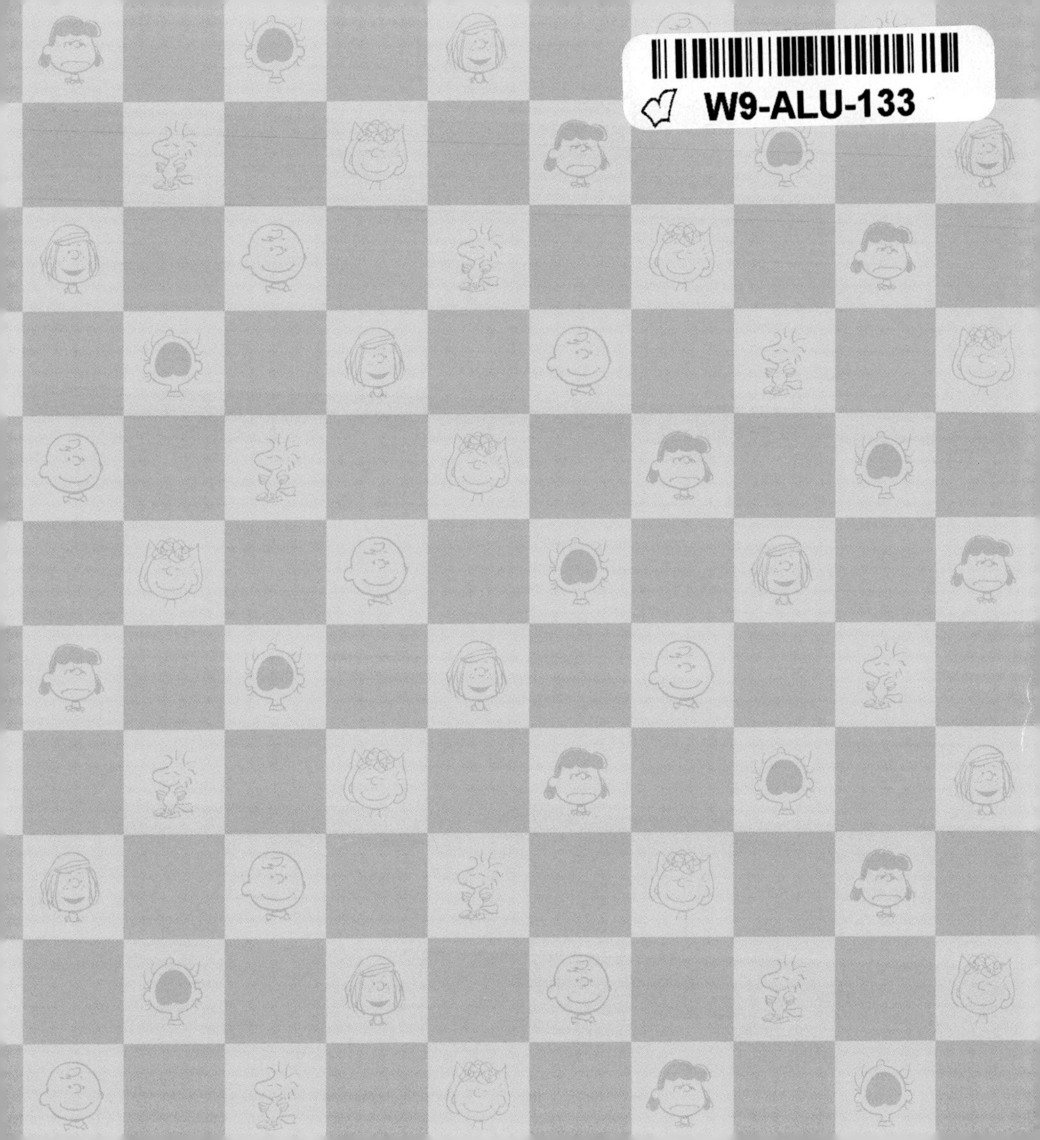

Good Grief, It's Your Birthday!

GROWING UP WITHOUT GROWING OLD

Cover and internal design by Michael Franck

Published by Sourcebooks, Inc.
P.O. Box 4410, Naperville, Illinois 60567-4410
(630) 961-3900
Fax: (630) 961-2168

www.sourcebooks.com

Library of Congress Cataloging-in-Publication data is on file with the publisher.

Printed and bound in the United States of America.

WOZ 10 9 8 7 6 5 4 3

Good Grief, It's Your Birthday!

✿ GROWING UP WITHOUT GROWING OLD ✿

Based on the comic strip, PEANUTS, by Charles M. Schulz

sourcebooks

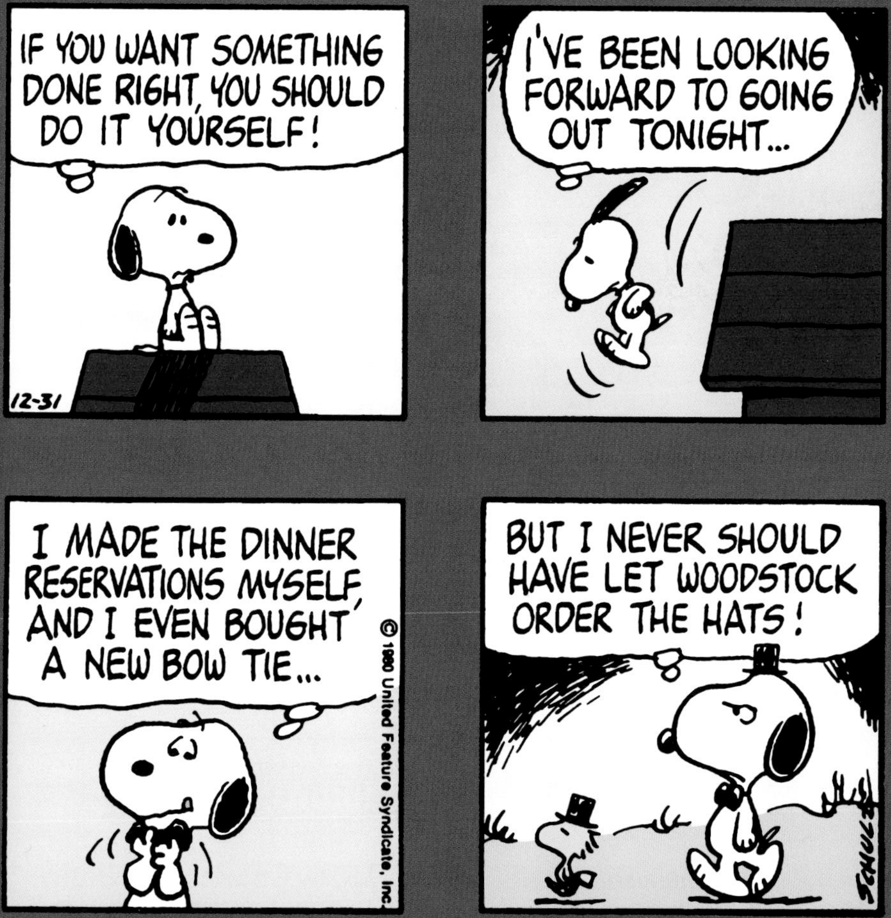
IF YOU WANT SOMETHING DONE RIGHT, YOU SHOULD DO IT YOURSELF!
12-31
I'VE BEEN LOOKING FORWARD TO GOING OUT TONIGHT...
I MADE THE DINNER RESERVATIONS MYSELF, AND I EVEN BOUGHT A NEW BOW TIE...
© 1980 United Feature Syndicate, Inc.
BUT I NEVER SHOULD HAVE LET WOODSTOCK ORDER THE HATS!
SCHULZ

Birthdays

are

good for you.

Statistics show that the
people who have the most
live the longest.

— **Larry Lorenzoni**

People shouldn't be

embarrassed

just because they get
caught acting a little

silly.

— **Charles Schulz**

Recall it as often as you wish,
a happy memory
never wears out.

— **Libbie Fudim**

You only live once...
but if you live it right,
once is enough.

— Joe E. Lewis

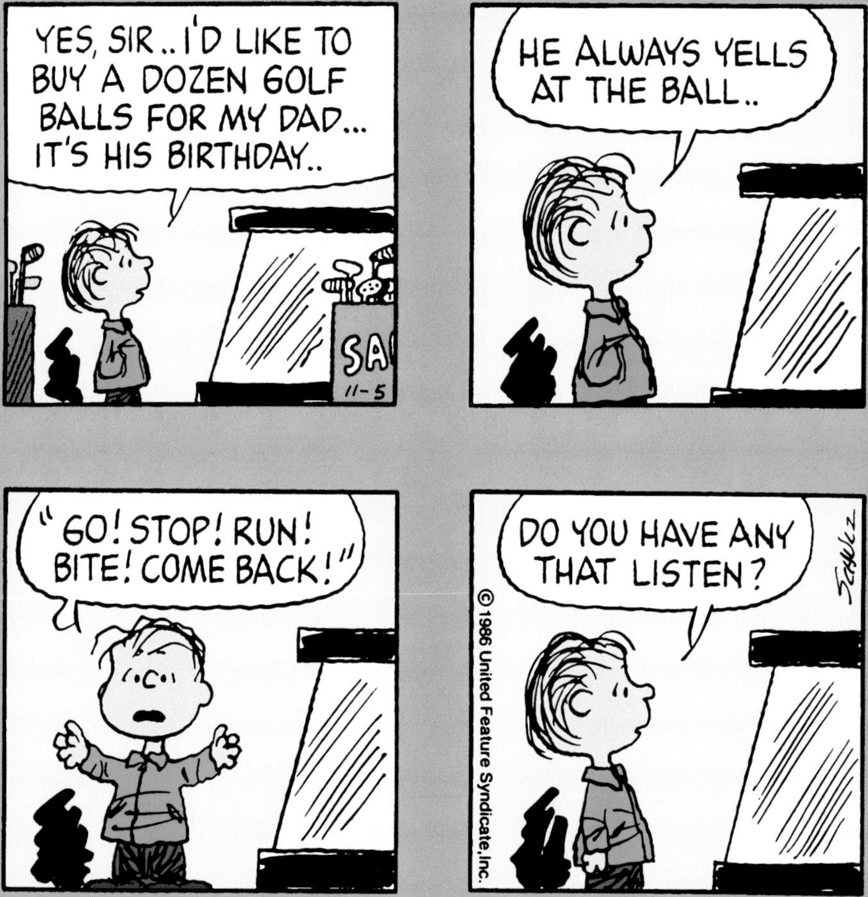
YES, SIR.. I'D LIKE TO BUY A DOZEN GOLF BALLS FOR MY DAD... IT'S HIS BIRTHDAY..
SA
11-5
HE ALWAYS YELLS AT THE BALL..
"GO! STOP! RUN! BITE! COME BACK!"
DO YOU HAVE ANY THAT LISTEN?
SCHULZ
© 1986 United Feature Syndicate, Inc.

Youth is when you blame all your troubles on your **parents; maturity** is when you learn that everything is the fault of the **younger generation.**

— Harold Coffin

The only
real way
to look younger is
not to be born so soon.

— **Charles Schulz**

Youth
is a circumstance you
can't do anything about.
The trick is to grow up
without getting old.

— **Frank Lloyd Wright**

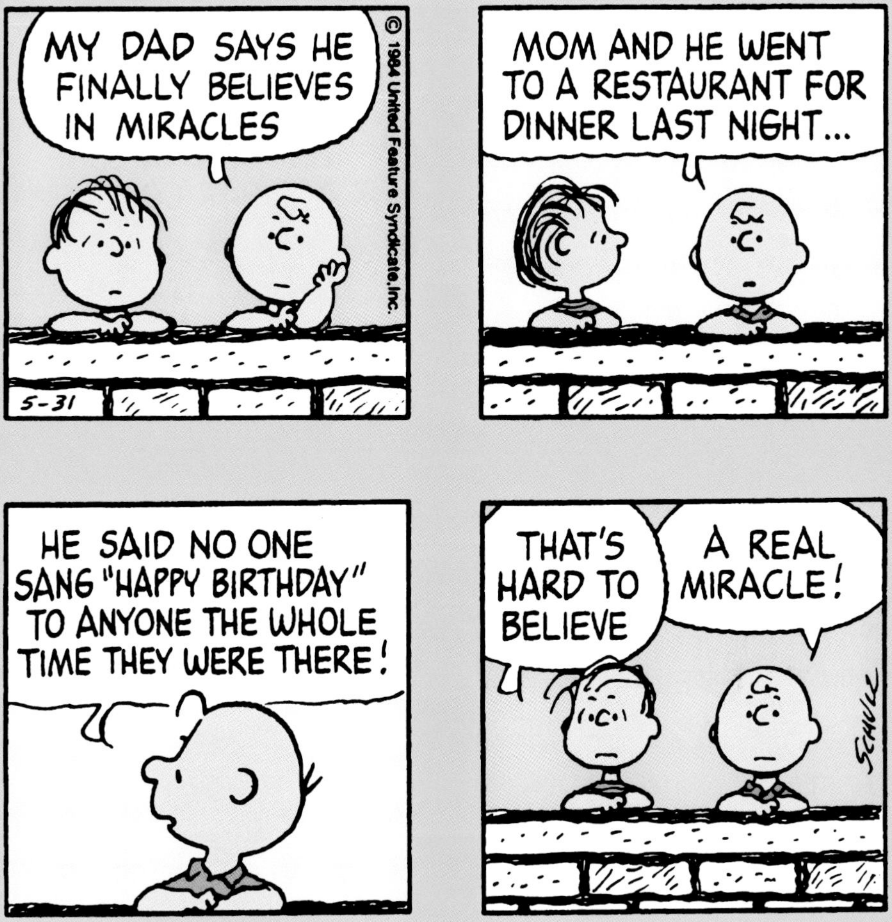
MY DAD SAYS HE FINALLY BELIEVES IN MIRACLES
© 1984 United Feature Syndicate, Inc.
5-31
MOM AND HE WENT TO A RESTAURANT FOR DINNER LAST NIGHT...
HE SAID NO ONE SANG "HAPPY BIRTHDAY" TO ANYONE THE WHOLE TIME THEY WERE THERE!
THAT'S HARD TO BELIEVE
A REAL MIRACLE!
SCHULZ

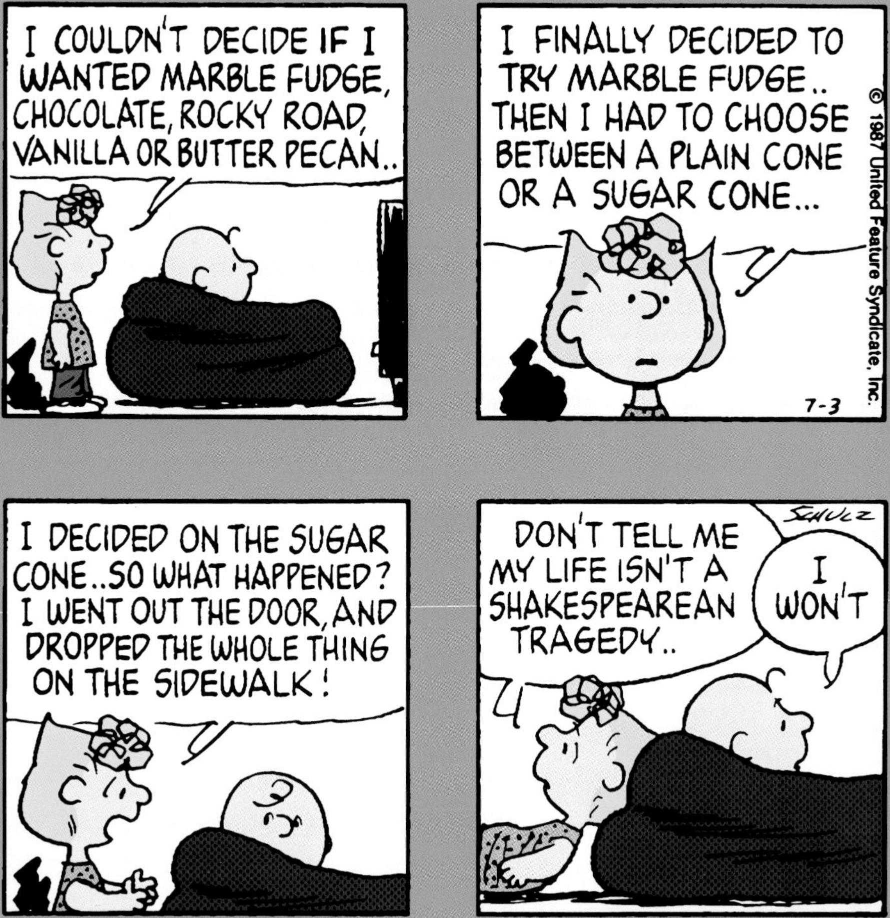
I COULDN'T DECIDE IF I WANTED MARBLE FUDGE, CHOCOLATE, ROCKY ROAD, VANILLA OR BUTTER PECAN..
I FINALLY DECIDED TO TRY MARBLE FUDGE.. THEN I HAD TO CHOOSE BETWEEN A PLAIN CONE OR A SUGAR CONE...
© 1987 United Feature Syndicate, Inc.
7-3
I DECIDED ON THE SUGAR CONE..SO WHAT HAPPENED? I WENT OUT THE DOOR, AND DROPPED THE WHOLE THING ON THE SIDEWALK!
SCHULZ
DON'T TELL ME MY LIFE ISN'T A SHAKESPEAREAN TRAGEDY..
I WON'T

Life
is like an
ice-cream cone,
you have to lick it one day at a time.

— **Charles Schulz**

Learn from yesterday, live for today, look to tomorrow, rest this afternoon.

— **Charles Schulz**

Be yourself.

No one can say you're doing it wrong.

— Charles Schulz

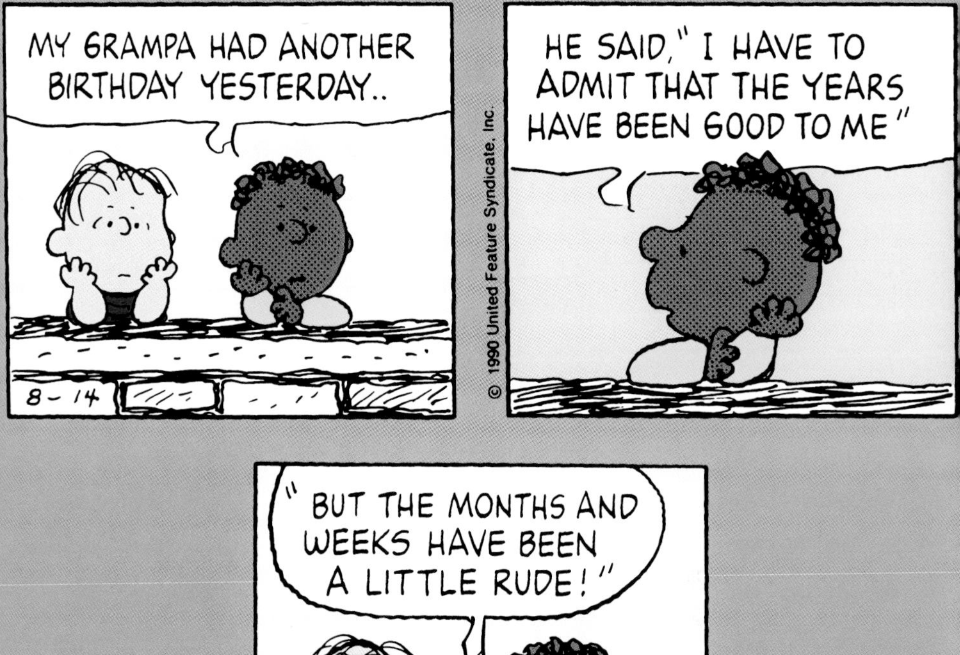
MY GRAMPA HAD ANOTHER BIRTHDAY YESTERDAY..
8-14
HE SAID, "I HAVE TO ADMIT THAT THE YEARS HAVE BEEN GOOD TO ME"
"BUT THE MONTHS AND WEEKS HAVE BEEN A LITTLE RUDE!"
SCHULZ

You can't help getting older, but **you don't have to get old.**

— George Burns

Aging
seems to be the
only available way
to live a long life.

— Kitty O'Neill Collins

People rarely succeed
unless they
have fun
in what they are doing.

— **Dale Carnegie**

I don't fool with
a lot of things
I can't have fun with.
There's not much reward in that.

— **Levon Helm**

No party is any fun unless
seasoned with folly.

— **Desiderius Erasmus**

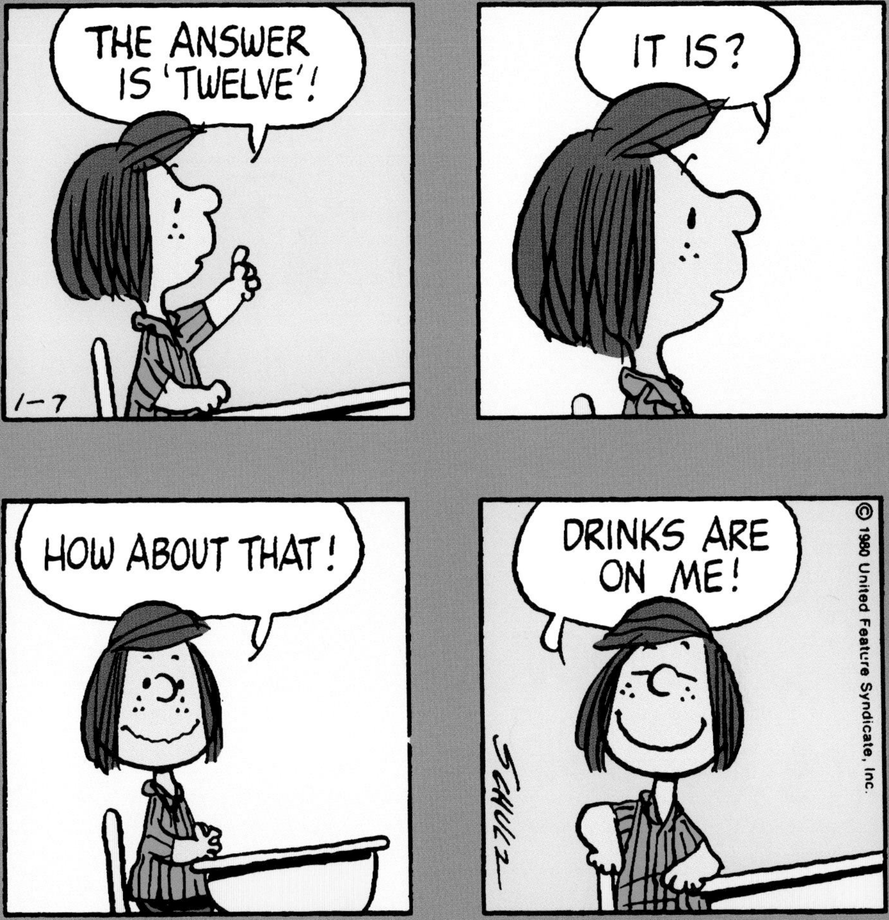

THE ANSWER IS 'TWELVE'!
1-7
IT IS?
HOW ABOUT THAT!
DRINKS ARE ON ME!
SCHULZ
© 1980 United Feature Syndicate, Inc.

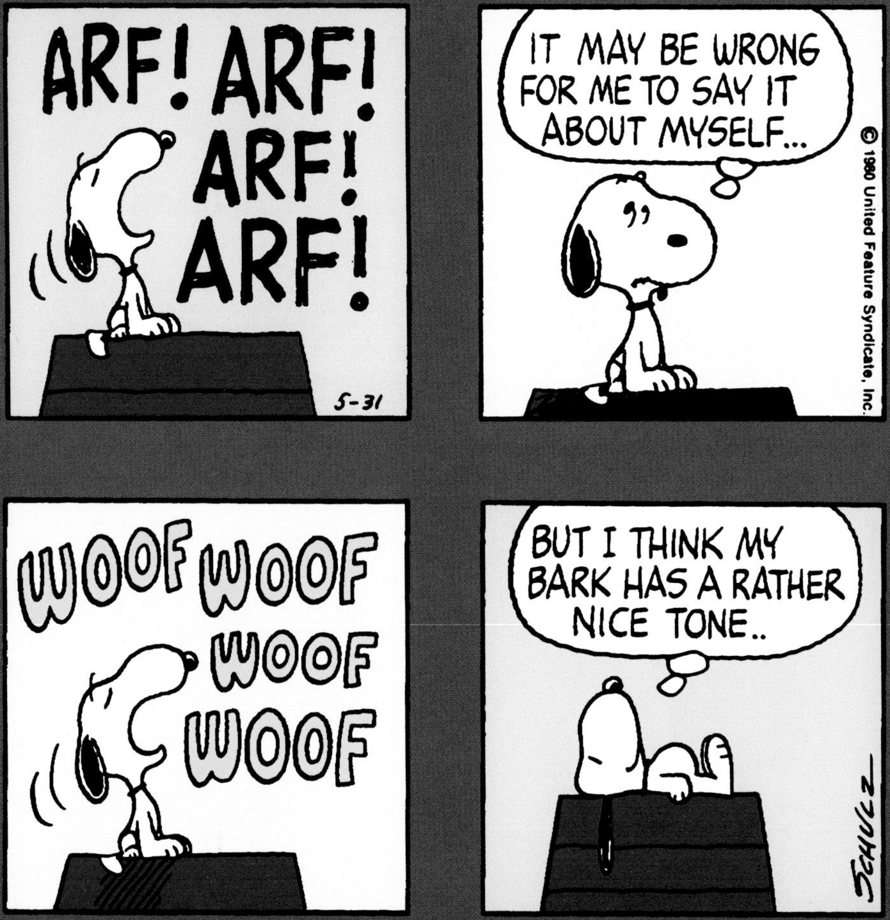
ARF! ARF! ARF! ARF!
5-31
IT MAY BE WRONG FOR ME TO SAY IT ABOUT MYSELF...
© 1980 United Feature Syndicate, Inc.
WOOF WOOF WOOF WOOF
BUT I THINK MY BARK HAS A RATHER NICE TONE..
SCHULZ

The **greatest** thing in the world is to know how to **belong to oneself.**

— **Michel de Montaigne**

I never loved another person **the way I loved myself.**

— **Mae West**

If you
carry your childhood
with you, you never become older.

— **Abraham Sutzkever**

Remember,
the greatest gift
is not found in a store nor
under a tree, but in the hearts
of true friends.

— **Cindy Lew**

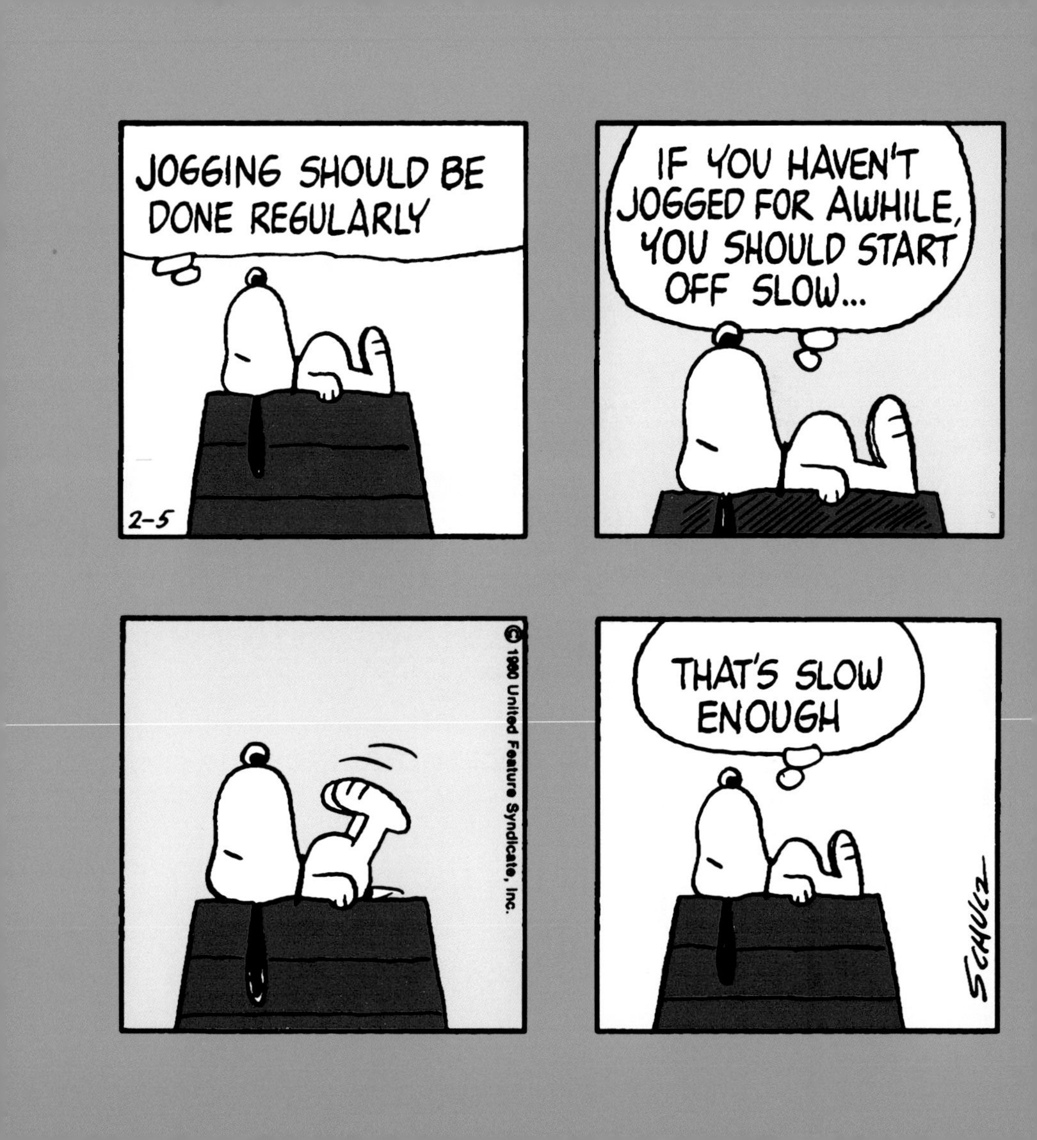
JOGGING SHOULD BE DONE REGULARLY
2-5
IF YOU HAVEN'T JOGGED FOR AWHILE, YOU SHOULD START OFF SLOW...
© 1980 United Feature Syndicate, Inc.
THAT'S SLOW ENOUGH
SCHULZ

Life would be infinitely happier
if we could only be born at
the age of eighty
and gradually approach
eighteen.

— **Mark Twain**

Whenever you find
yourself on the side of the
majority,
it is time to
pause and reflect.

— Mark Twain

In order to be
irreplaceable, one must
always be different.

— Coco Chanel

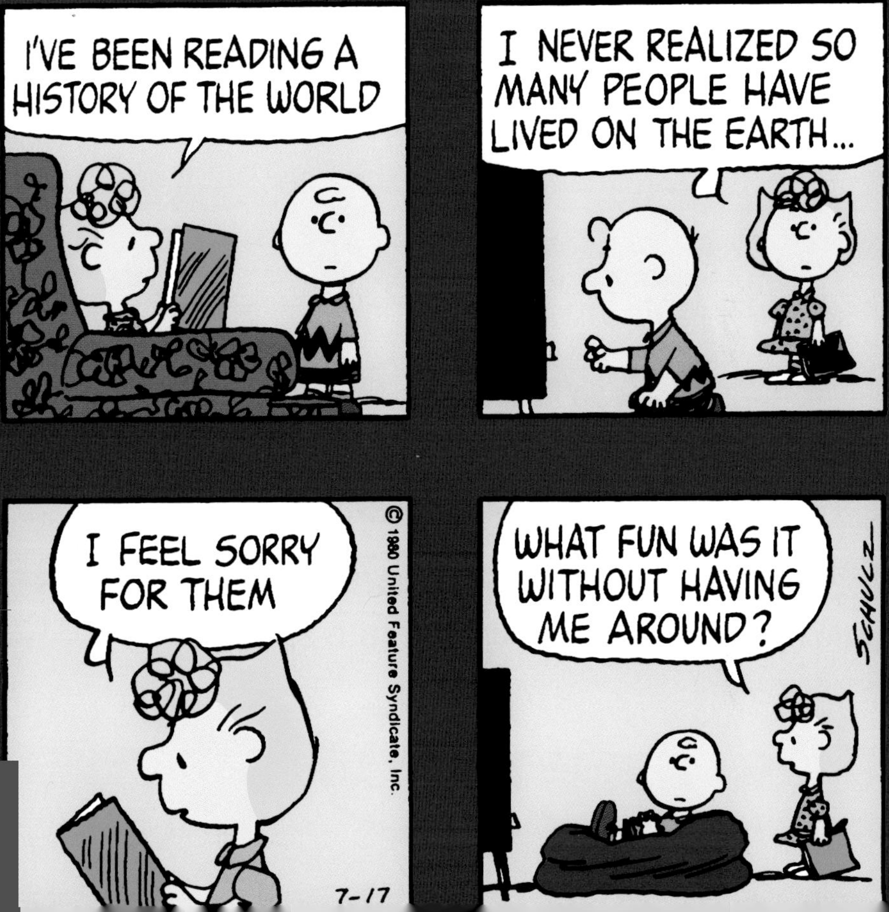
I'VE BEEN READING A HISTORY OF THE WORLD
I NEVER REALIZED SO MANY PEOPLE HAVE LIVED ON THE EARTH...
I FEEL SORRY FOR THEM
© 1980 United Feature Syndicate, Inc.
7-17
WHAT FUN WAS IT WITHOUT HAVING ME AROUND?
SCHULZ

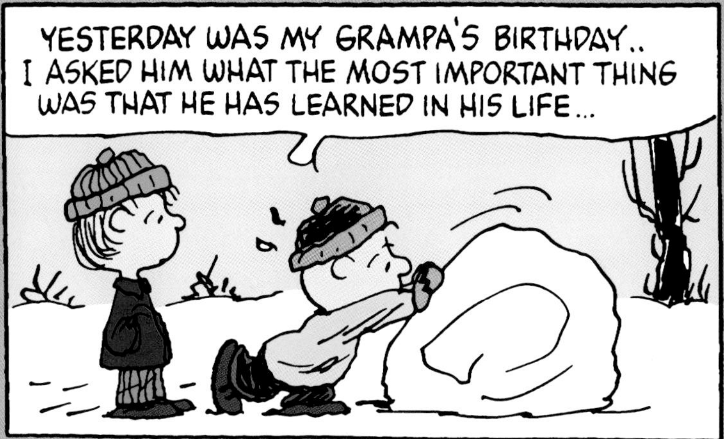
YESTERDAY WAS MY GRAMPA'S BIRTHDAY.. I ASKED HIM WHAT THE MOST IMPORTANT THING WAS THAT HE HAS LEARNED IN HIS LIFE...
© 1988 United Feature Syndicate, Inc.

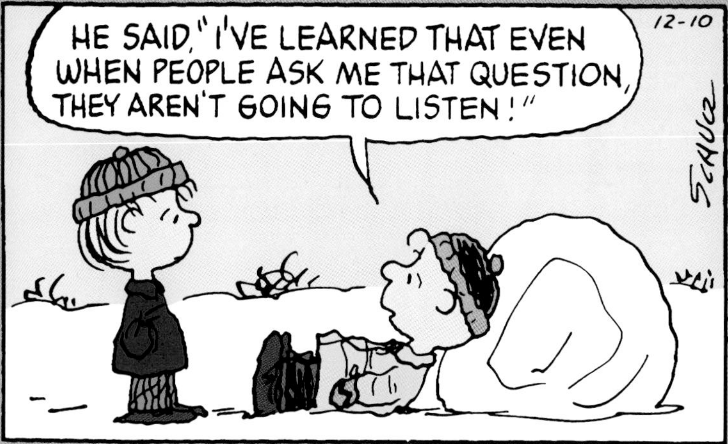
12-10
HE SAID, "I'VE LEARNED THAT EVEN WHEN PEOPLE ASK ME THAT QUESTION, THEY AREN'T GOING TO LISTEN!"
SCHULZ

Experience
is not what happens to you;
it's what you do
with what happens to you.

— **Aldous Huxley**

A word to the wise
ain't necessary—it's the
stupid ones
that need advice.

— **Bill Cosby**

My grandmother started walking
five miles a day when she was sixty.
She's ninety-seven now, and we don't know
where the hell she is.

— **Ellen DeGeneres**

It takes half your life
before you discover life is a
do-it-yourself project.

— **Napoleon Hill**

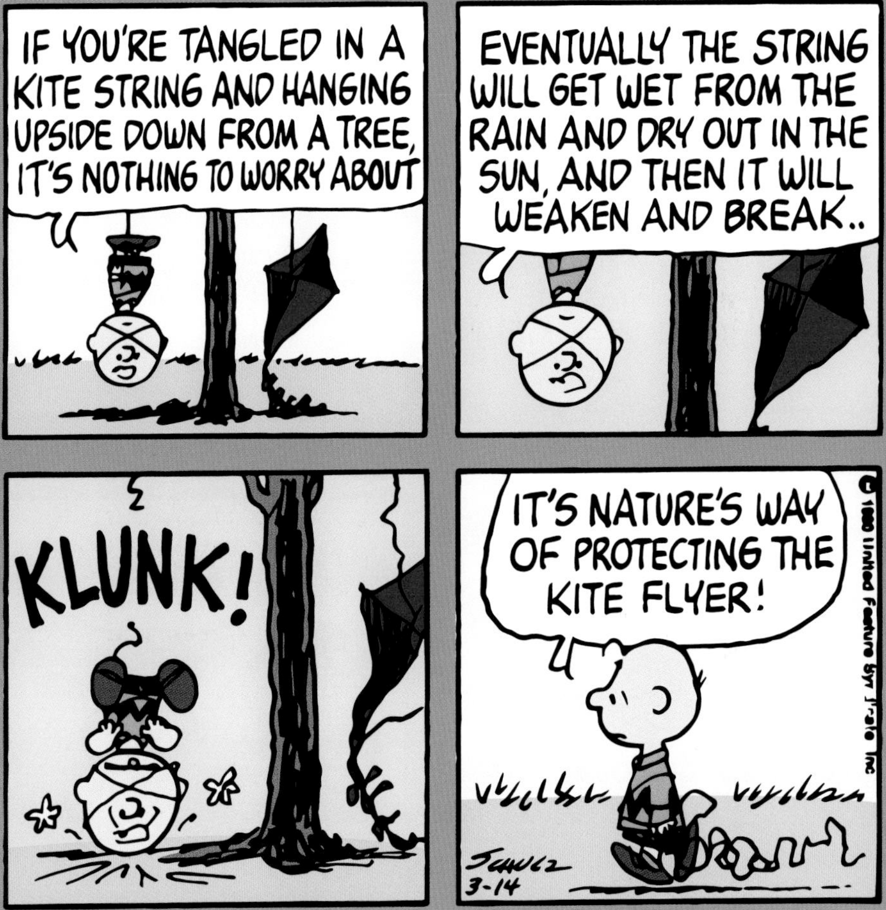
IF YOU'RE TANGLED IN A KITE STRING AND HANGING UPSIDE DOWN FROM A TREE, IT'S NOTHING TO WORRY ABOUT
EVENTUALLY THE STRING WILL GET WET FROM THE RAIN AND DRY OUT IN THE SUN, AND THEN IT WILL WEAKEN AND BREAK..
KLUNK!
IT'S NATURE'S WAY OF PROTECTING THE KITE FLYER!
© 1980 United Feature Syndicate Inc
SCHULZ
3-14

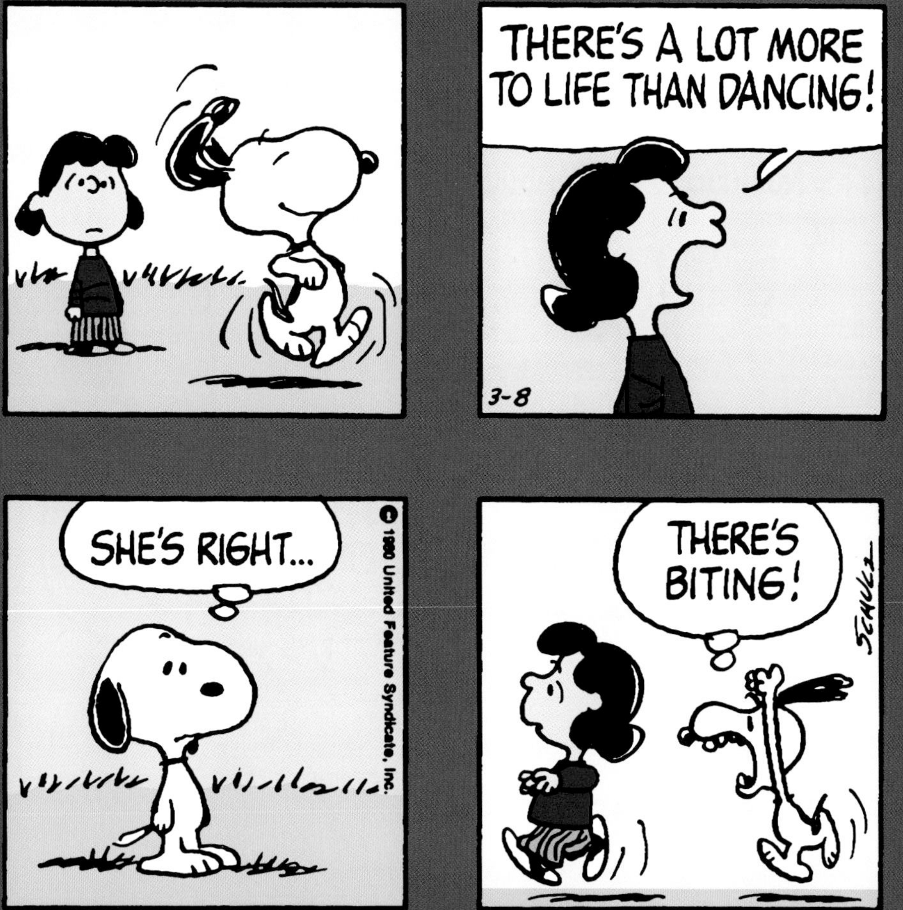
THERE'S A LOT MORE TO LIFE THAN DANCING!
3-8
SHE'S RIGHT...
© 1980 United Feature Syndicate, Inc.
THERE'S BITING!
SCHULZ

We are always the
same age inside.
— **Gertrude Stein**

It takes a long time to
grow young.
— **Pablo Picasso**

To *dance*
is to *live!*
— **Charles Schulz**

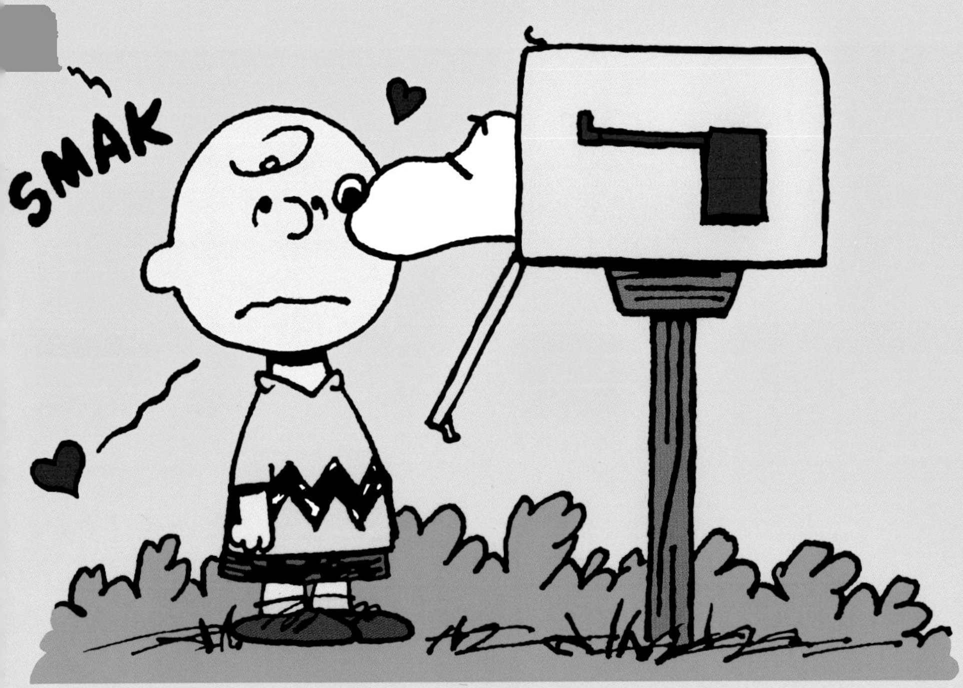
SMAK

A true friend
remembers your
birthday but **not your age.**

— **Anonymous**

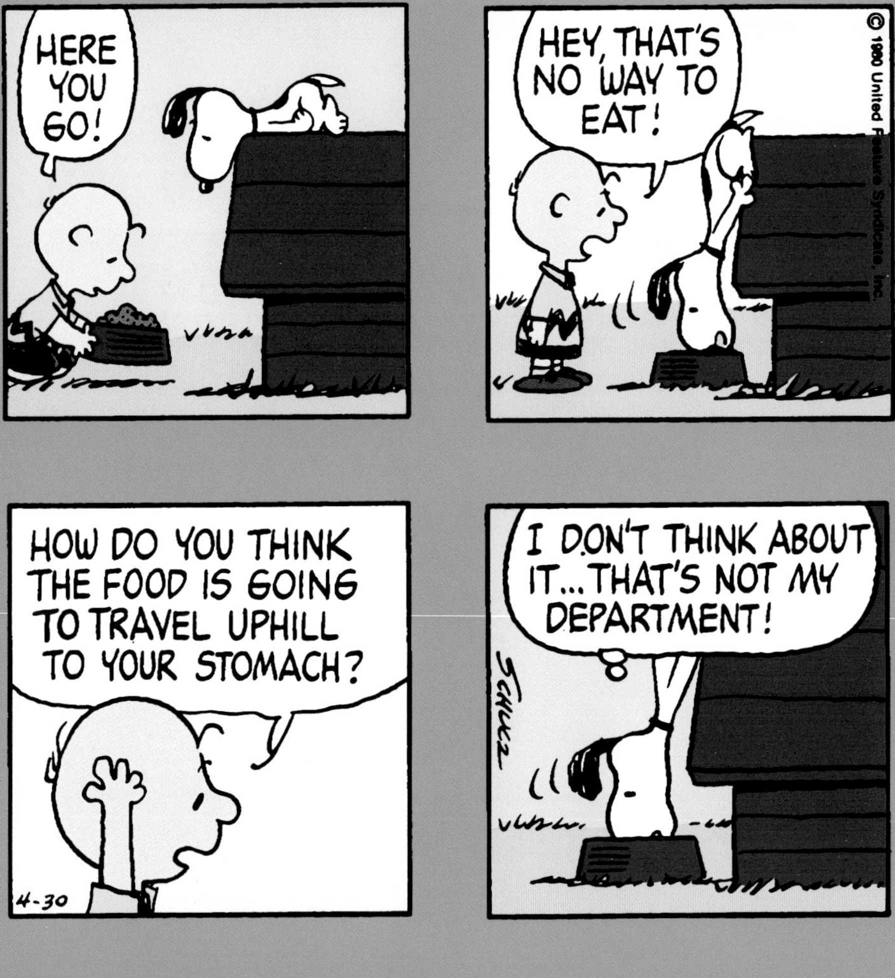
HERE YOU GO!
HEY, THAT'S NO WAY TO EAT!
© 1980 United Feature Syndicate, Inc.
HOW DO YOU THINK THE FOOD IS GOING TO TRAVEL UPHILL TO YOUR STOMACH?
4-30
I DON'T THINK ABOUT IT... THAT'S NOT MY DEPARTMENT!
SCHULZ

Birthdays are nature's
way of telling us to
eat more cake.

— **Anonymous**

When someone asks if you'd like
cake or pie,
why not say you want
cake and pie?

— **Lisa Loeb**

Let's face it, a
nice creamy chocolate cake
does a lot for a lot of people;
it does for me.

— **Audrey Hepburn**

Just remember, when you're
over the hill,
you begin to
pick up speed.
— **Charles Schulz**

Happiness is
good health
and a
bad memory.
— **Ingrid Bergman**

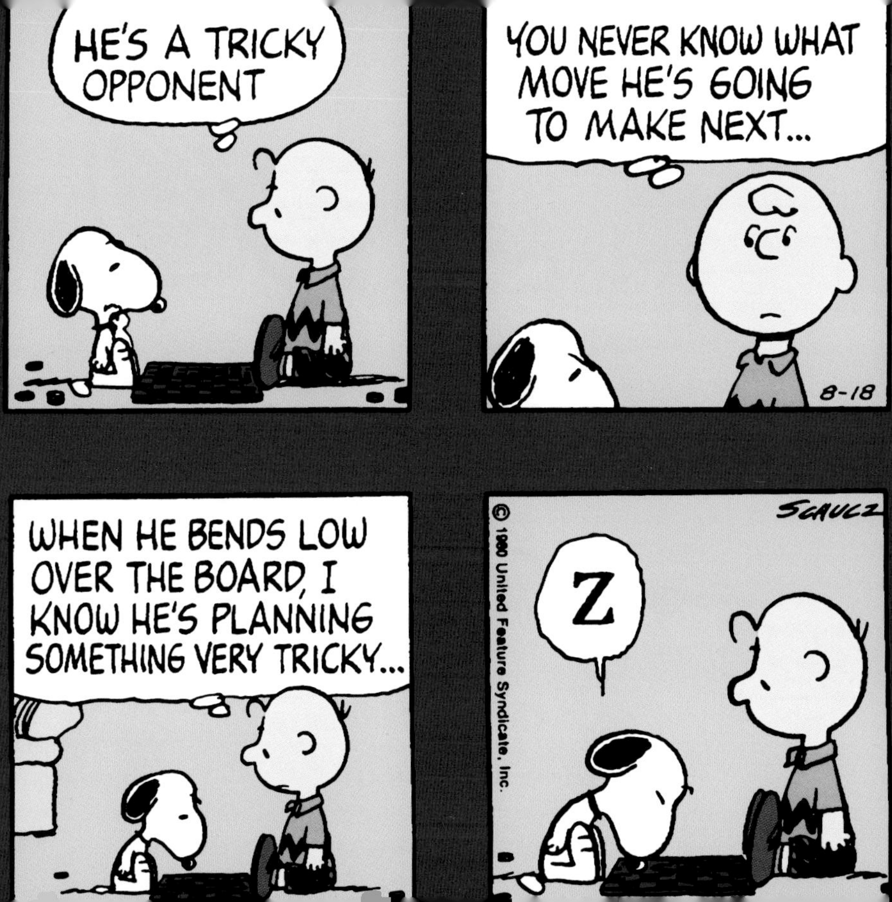
HE'S A TRICKY OPPONENT
YOU NEVER KNOW WHAT MOVE HE'S GOING TO MAKE NEXT...
8-18
WHEN HE BENDS LOW OVER THE BOARD, I KNOW HE'S PLANNING SOMETHING VERY TRICKY...
© 1980 United Feature Syndicate, Inc.
Z

Each day
provides its own
gifts.

— Marcus Aurelius